MARY CASSATT
GRAPHIC ART

MARY CASSATT

GRAPHIC ART

Adelyn Dohme Breeskin

PUBLISHED FOR SMITHSONIAN INSTITUTION TRAVELING

EXHIBITION SERVICE BY SMITHSONIAN INSTITUTION PRESS

WASHINGTON, D.C., 1981

Library of Congress Cataloging in Publication Data
Breeskin, Adelyn Dohme, 1896-
Mary Cassatt : graphic art.
Catalog of a traveling exhibition to be shown in
6 U.S. museums.
1. Cassatt, Mary, 1844-1926—Exhibitions.
I. Smithsonian Institution. Traveling Exhibition
Service.
NE539.C3A4   1981   769.92'4   80-28507
ISBN 0-86528-006-1

Cover: *Afternoon Tea Party*, c. 1891. Color print with drypoint, soft-ground,
and aquatint. 13½ x 10⅜ (34.2 x 26.3). BR 151, fourth and
final state. Lent by The Saint Louis Art Museum for the first four
showings and the National Gallery of Art for the last two showings. Catalog number 39.

Frontispiece: *The Fitting*, c. 1891. Color print with drypoint and soft-ground.
14¾ x 10⅛ (37.7 x 25.7). BR 147, sixth and final state.
Anonymous lender. Catalog number 35.

Exhibiting Institutions
March 1981–May 1982

Amon Carter Museum Fort Worth, Texas	The Saint Louis Art Museum Saint Louis, Missouri
Virginia Museum of Fine Arts Richmond, Virginia	Grand Rapids Art Museum Grand Rapids, Michigan
New Orleans Museum of Art New Orleans, Louisiana	Museum of Art, Carnegie Institute Pittsburgh, Pennsylvania

Contents

The Letter c. 1891   Color print with drypoint, soft-ground, and aquatint (on blouse)
13⅝ x 8¹⁵⁄₁₆ (34.4 x 22.6)   BR 146, third and final state   Anonymous lender   [cat. 34]

Foreword

My feeling for Mary Cassatt devolves from the strong feelings of tenderness and innocence that she conveys. She treats her subjects with a special gentleness and warmth, a genuine understanding unique in painters of this or any other period. Her impressionism is one, not of saccharin, but of genuine sweetness combined with an objectivity that belies over-sentimentality.

Her strength was that of America itself, open and honest, and these she portrayed with a palette that was light, airy, and full of sunshine, evoking an aura of bright noonday color as in a southern clime. Her colors are never dazzling but muted, thereby enhancing the tenderness conveyed by her subtle brush. Although she worked in Paris throughout her career, the artist's subjects, including those of family life portrayed in this exhibition of prints, are bound to the American character. "She remains exclusively of her people," wrote an art critic of the era, an observation Cassatt herself endorsed in a statement to her biographer: "I am an American, simply and frankly American."

For all her American approach to her art, many of her prints show a strong Oriental influence, popular in the Paris of her day where there was an influential vogue for Japanese art. This simplicity and directness of line adds an element of great strength to her work in this lighter medium, strengthening the conviction of essential warmth that her character must have conveyed.

Sadly the work of Cassatt, as the case with so many possessing foresight and the spirit of independence, was not accepted in America for many years, this despite the themes of family life, affection, and her keen observations of the special relationships between mother and child.

Perhaps it was the lack of sentimentality in her work—paintings devoid of customary prettiness—that explained why they were unaccepted by popular taste during her lifetime. Cassatt's view was personal, yet passionate, an honest recording of her subjects in a style of precision and elegance. Today, of course, we view Cassatt's art with interest, and appreciation and affection.

This collection of Mary Cassatt's graphic art, chosen by Adelyn Dohme Breeskin, the world authority on the painter, for the Smithsonian Institution Traveling Exhibition Service, reflects an appreciation not only for the skill and creativity of Mary Cassatt but also for her contribution to the landscape of art and the maturation of American cultural tastes, the twin lifelong interests of the only American to work within the nineteenth-century Impressionist tradition. Through the imaginative effort of SITES, people from one end of the United States to the other will be able to see the graphic works of this remarkable woman who early on sensed the need for fine works of art that would enrich American life.

S. Dillon Ripley, Secretary, Smithsonian Institution

Acknowledgments

There has not been an exhibition of the graphic work of Mary Cassatt in well over a decade that surveys so completely Miss Cassatt's variety of techniques and synthesis of styles. The Smithsonian Institution Traveling Exhibition Service is indebted to Adelyn Dohme Breeskin for graciously consenting to select this exhibition and for contributing her important essay on Mary Cassatt. A note of special thanks is due to S. Dillon Ripley, Secretary of the Smithsonian Institution, for his foreword to the catalog and to Donald McClelland, sites exhibition coordinator, who provided considerable scholarly as well as administrative support in the organization of this important exhibition. In addition, specific thanks are due the following members of sites staff: Emily Dyer, registrar; Matou Goodwin, secretary; Eileen Harakal, public information coordinator; and Andrea Stevens, publications coordinator.

Many persons have been helpful in securing loans, providing information and material for the catalog, and aiding in the organization of the exhibition. Among these, we especially thank the following:

Ripley F. Albright, assistant curator, Prints and Drawings, Brooklyn Museum

Gene Baro, consulting curator, Prints and Drawings, Brooklyn Museum

Karen Beall, curator, Prints, Library of Congress

Charles Cathey, registrar, Museum of Art, Carnegie Institute

Miss Laura Carson, curator, Treat Gallery, Bates College

Sylvan Cole, director, Associated American Artists

Miss Elaine Evans Dee, curator, Drawings and Prints, Cooper-Hewitt Museum of Design and Decorative Arts

Rowland P. Elzea, associate director, Delaware Art Museum

Jay Fisher, associate curator, Prints, Drawings, and Photography, The Baltimore Museum of Art

John Freshour, registrar, Library of Congress

John Ittman, curator, Prints and Drawings, Minneapolis Museum of Art

Harold Joachim, curator, Drawings and Prints, The Art Institute of Chicago

Miss Francis Follin Jones, curator, Collections, The Art Museum, Princeton University

Martin Krause, curator, Prints and Drawings, Indianapolis Museum of Art

John Lane, director, Museum of Art, Carnegie Institute

Mrs. Jan Keene Muhlert, director, Amon Carter Museum of Western Art

Robert M. Murdock, director, Grand Rapids Art Museum

Miss Mary Riordan, director, The Hackley Art Museum

Greg G. Thielen, curator, Springfield Art Museum

Miss Christine Swenson, assistant curator, Prints and Drawings, Smith College Museum of Art

Andrew Robison, curator, Prints and Drawings, National Gallery of Art

There are many other individuals and institutions across the country that will work with SITES as they host *Mary Cassatt: Graphic Art*. It is a pleasure for us to be able to present such an exhibition to what we know will be a large and enthusiastic audience.

Peggy A. Loar, Director, SITES

Lenders to the Exhibition

Amon Carter Museum, Fort Worth, Texas

Art Institute of Chicago, Illinois

The Art Museum, Princeton University, New Jersey

Associated American Artists, New York

Baltimore Museum of Art, Maryland

Adelyn D. Breeskin, Washington, D.C.

Brooklyn Museum, New York

Cooper-Hewitt Museum
of Design and Decorative Arts, New York

Delaware Art Museum, Wilmington

Georgia Museum of Art, the University of Georgia

Grand Rapids Art Museum, Michigan

Hackley Art Museum, Muskegon, Michigan

Indianapolis Museum of Art, Indiana

Library of Congress

Minneapolis Institute of Art, Minnesota

Museum of Art, Carnegie Institute, Pittsburgh, Pennsylvania

National Gallery of Art, Chester Dale Collection, Washington, D.C.

New York Public Library

The Saint Louis Art Museum, Missouri

Smith College Museum of Art, Northampton, Massachusetts

Springfield Art Museum, Massachusetts

Treat Gallery, Bates College, Lewiston, Maine

Maternal Caress   c. 1891   Color print with drypoint and soft-ground   14½ x 10⁹⁄₁₆ (36.7 x 26.8)
BR 150, third and final state   Lent by Amon Carter Museum   [cat. 38]

MARY CASSATT: GRAPHIC ART

Adelyn Dohme Breeskin

Mary Cassatt defied the conventions of her day by going to Europe after completing a four-year course at the Pennsylvania Academy of Fine Arts. This was in the 1860s, and there were no public art museums in America in which an aspiring art student could study works by the old masters. Despite parental protests, at the age of twenty-two, she left for Paris in 1866 to copy and study paintings at the Louvre and to attend the art class of Charles Chaplin as well as that of Paul Soyer and the other teachers at Ecouen near Paris.

After some four years of concentrated study the Franco-Prussian War began and, at her parents insistence, she came home for about a year and a half. On her return to Europe in 1872, she first visited Parma, Italy, to examine the murals by Correggio in the church of San Giovanni Evangelista. She remained in Parma for eight months where she rented studio space from Carlo Raimondi, the teacher of engraving and etching at the local university. In all probability, she took lessons from him in etching since her earliest print in this exhibition—*Costume Study after Gavarni* [cat. 1]—already shows a knowledge of print techniques.

From Parma, Cassatt went on to Rome, followed by trips to Spain, and the cities of Antwerp and Haarlem before settling again in Paris which then became her home. In 1877, Edgar Degas came with a mutual friend, Joseph Tourney, to ask her to join their group of painters, sculptors, and gravers later known as the Impressionists—an invitation she accepted with delight. Her relationship with Degas became very congenial, and he gave her work most helpful criticism.

Her parents and older sister had been living with Cassatt in Paris since 1877 and after she and her family returned from a summer spent near Paris at Marly-le-Roi in 1880, Degas wrote his friend Henri Rouart: "The Cassatts have come back from Marly-le-Roi; Mlle. is installed in a studio on the street level which [it] seems to me is not very healthy. What she did in the country looks very well in studio light. It is much more firm and more noble than what she did last year." [1]

During the preceding year, 1879, Degas had approached both Cassatt and Pissarro and asked them to join him in publishing a journal of original prints to be called *Le Jour et La Nuit*. "That" he said, "will teach us all to draw." This invitation stimulated Cassatt to produce prints worthy of her association with these two eminent artist friends.

Degas wrote to his friend, the etcher Bracquemond: "We have made some experiments. . . . Mlle. Cassatt is in the midst of some at this moment." Indeed, it seems apparent that she immediately became partial to the use of soft-ground rather than aquatint for tone. It was a technique that had been used during the eighteenth century in France by artists such as Desboucourt and continued to be used by English artists such as Constable and Girtin; however, it was overlooked in France, with the dominant use of aquatint taking its place. Sometimes Cassatt combined these, as in the 1879 print called *The Corner of the Sofa* (no. 3) [cat. 2]. We know that *In the Opera Box* (no. 3) [cat. 3] was definitely done for the journal, a handsome print based on a similar composition of her first painting shown in the 1879 Impressionist exhibition. Another print at least partly prepared for the journal was even more experimental. Called *The Visitor* [cat. 8], according to a note on one impression in Miss Cassatt's handwriting it went into thirteen states, seven of which I have termed unrecorded trial proofs. It is also a very handsome composition with the large central figure partly silhouetted against the lightly curtained window in the background. The seated figure at the right was drawn with a blunt tool, possibly the point of the handle of a brush, directly into the soft-ground rather than being drawn on the paper covering the soft-ground.

Following this, Cassatt produced one of two dark soft-ground prints [cat. 6 and 7] of her mother in the library with bookcases in the background. Catalog number 6 is shown in the third state. This plate was brought out of the studio closet in 1923 and given to the younger Delâtre for restriking in nine impressions. Also, in 1880, she produced her only lithograph [cat. 4] done directly on stone. She did not care sufficiently for the medium to use it after that except for one done on transfer paper in 1904. She preferred the use of soft-ground as demonstrated in one other *Lady in Black, in a Loge, Facing Right* [cat. 5].

Mary Cassatt always kept in close touch with her American friends, so there are few French people among her models; however, Mlle Luguet—as this diminutive little girl was called—was the daughter of the woman who taught French to Cassatt's nieces during their long winter's stay with the artist and her parents. In a few of her drypoints on which she concentrated after about 1882, there is but one print, *Susan Seated before a Row of Trees* [cat. 10] in which she introduced some etching with drypoint. At the same time, she continued experimenting with soft-ground and aquatint. In *Nurse and Baby Bill* (no. 2) [cat. 15], she pressed netting into her soft-ground giving a much more regular pattern of tone than would be possible with aquatint.

The last portrait of the artist's mother done in 1889 [cat. 18] in soft-ground and aquatint follows the same composition found in the large painted version of it. Here, as in the painting, old age is given a most sympathetic reading with an eloquent sense of resignation and quietude. Mrs. Cassatt lived five years longer in spite of a weak heart and severe arthritis.

Between 1889 and 1891 Mary Cassatt created a series of twelve drypoints for publication, with twenty-five impressions of each. This series was the first that Cassatt made for publication, except for *In the Opera Box* (no. 3) of which fifty impressions were printed and three others with twenty-five impressions of each. The remaining 123 plates made before 1889 were all made as practice in learning to draw, as Degas had suggested; very few impressions were printed and at least six of them were done on the backs of already used plates. In the margins of some, there is a written note in her handwriting, "only 3 proofs taken" or "4 proofs." The series of twelve drypoints, however, were done for exhibition with twenty-five impressions of each and all were included in her large show at the Galerie Durand-Ruel in 1893 in Paris.

Two years later at the Durand-Ruel branch in New York City where they were shown, almost none were sold. This experience caused her to write to M. Durand-Ruel how disappointed she was "that my compatriots have so little liking for any of my work." The set is equally divided between mothers and their babies and studies of young girls or young women. The first is *The Map* [cat. 19], also called *The Lesson*, in which two girls are seated leaning over a table studying a map. The tonality is deep, with rich shadows and brilliant light playing on their features. The grouping of the two is composed with economy and they form a lovely arabesque with the dominant curve of the table. In strong contrast is *Baby's Back* [cat. 20]. In it, the delicacy of the shading is such that it appears as though breathed onto the plate. To heighten the concentration on this little body, the mother's face is mostly hidden and her hands are merely suggested. The very finely textured toning of the flesh tones demanded constant reenforcing, a necessity often found in Cassatt's rendering of shading on faces and hair throughout her drypoint work.

In her prints which are closely related to her paintings, I once stated that I thought that the prints followed rather than preceded the paintings. Now I am not so sure. *The Stocking* [cat. 21] is the same composition—in reverse, of course—in pastel in the Gulbenkian collection in Lisbon. The pastel is more finished and has more detail and may very well have followed the drypoint. Cassatt noted on one impression of the print that the child was reaching out her arm toward a parrot which was on a perch in the room where she posed.

The Mandolin Player [cat. 22] is quite unique and is shown in its last and seventh state. It was Degas who told Cassatt to always place her people in their normal surroundings. Here, the player holds the mandolin as though she was actually playing it as she looks at the music on the stand; the hands are especially well done. She is seated on an upholstered settee in a room with a framed picture and a fan on the wall behind her. Together, they give a feeling of ambiance to a whole interior.

In *Reflection* [cat. 23], on the contrary, the attention is focused on the solemn face of the lady whose hat and upper part of her costume are dark. This sense of *Repose* is given in the following print [cat. 24] by the positions of the hands. It was the artist's companion-maid who looks at us as she holds the child's right hand while the child rests her left hand reposefully on Mathilde's arm. *Tea* [cat. 25] is a very handsome drypoint, with strong Japanese overtones. In the young lady's left hand is a large Japanese fan and on the table is one of the cups from the sparkling blue Cantonese tea set in Cassatt's *Lady at the Tea Table* at the Metropolitan Museum and in the colorprint entitled: *Afternoon Tea Party* [cat. 39]. In *Hélène of Septeuil* [cat. 26], there is the parrot that the child was reaching her arm toward in *The Stocking*. Hélène, in her big round hat, is about to feed the parrot a treat, as her mother's strong hand supports her. *Nursing* [cat. 27] is a picture of contentment on the part of this baby. Miss Cassatt had watched her sister-in-law nursing young Gardner often enough to recognize just how much babies could enjoy their repast.

Both Cassatt and Degas were fascinated by the mirror image as a means of extending space. In *The Mirror* [cat. 28] the reflection shows more of the mother's figure than is otherwise shown and makes one wonder how the artist could see so much of the chair. *The Bonnet* [cat. 29] also contains a mirror, but this time a hand mirror. As she tries on a new bonnet the charming young girl considers its purchase very seriously. The last of the series shows Mathilde once again holding *The Parrot* [cat. 30]. She holds its claws in her two capable hands and looks down at it. She sits in a straight back chair and her plaited dark blouse forms handsome, textured details, somewhat lighter than her very dark hair. *Quietude* [cat. 31] is not a part of the set of twelve drypoints, but it was done at the same time and is usually shown with them. It is, I think, the most popular of the artist's prints of the mother and child. One of Cassatt's close friends was Georges Clemenceau and during World War I he kept this print hanging in his office as a restful and happy note.

In 1890 Degas and Cassatt together visited the great Japanese exhibition at the Ecole des Beaux Arts. Both artists had already studied Japanese prints whenever they found them in Paris art shops. But their attention was now especially attracted to that comprehensive showing which amazed them by its novelty, its originality, and its different uses of basic art concepts. They absorbed it with true understanding of its intrinsic qualities. Cassatt bought a large number of the woodcuts which she then studied further until she succeeded in translating the Japanese woodcut technique into her series of ten great color prints. They became her most original contribution, adding a new chapter to the history of the graphic arts. She used, instead of wood blocks, copper plates with drypoint line over soft-ground or aquatint ground. In the series of ten color prints as a whole, the subject matter—as in the drypoint series—is divided between studies of women and the mother and child theme. The finest, in my opinion, is the draped nude called *Woman Bathing* (or *The Toilette*) [cat. 36]. In comparing it with a somewhat similar Japanese woodcut figure one can see how Cassatt found their secret of suggesting fully rounded contours by the subtle use of outlines. Upon seeing this print, Degas exclaimed that he would not admit that a woman was able to draw that well! Such draftmanship is indeed masterly, and it was evidently done directly from the model onto the copper without any preliminary sketches since none so far have been found.

The use of color throughout this series of color prints is most effective and varies considerably. The colors are drawn from Miss Cassatt's own palette rather than that used in Japanese prints where black is given a prominent place. As an Impressionist colorist, she avoided using black—instead, using dark browns, grays, blues, and greens and with them a wide range of pinks, light blue, yellow, and tan shades. The colors were always in flat areas without any shading. One amusing detail concerning the color prints is the fact that in some of them Miss Cassatt gave Japanese features to her models. In *The Letter* [cat. 34], for instance, the model looks quite Oriental as does the baby in *Maternal Caress* [cat. 38]. In *In The Omnibus* [cat. 33], the mother's head is handsomely described within the frame of one of the bus windows. The bold asymmetrical design is relieved by the river view shown through the windows. *The Fitting* [cat. 35] is a more simply constructed design of great beauty. The delightful standing figure looks down toward the stooping figure of the dressmaker whose solid form contrasts with the lithe slimness of the young girl in her evening dress of striped lavender and pink. Cassatt's set of ten color prints impressed Pissarro so deeply that in April 1861 he wrote to his son, Lucien:

> It is absolutely necessary, while what I saw yesterday at Miss Cassatt's is still fresh in mind, to tell you about the colored engravings she is to show at Durand-Ruel's at the same time as I.[2] . . .
>
> You remember the effects you strove for at Eragny? Well, Miss Cassatt has realized just such effects, and admirably; the tone even, subtle, delicate, without stains on seams; adorable blues, fresh rose, etc. . . . But the result is admirable, as beautiful as Japanese work, and it's done with printers ink![3]

In spite of the fact that these color prints did not sell well the artist received the applause of a few friends—including Pissarro and Degas as well as some critics and connoisseurs—enough to spur her on to continue working in the color print medium. She no longer used so much soft-ground; instead, she used aquatint on the later color prints such as *Gathering Fruit, Peasant Mother and Child,* and *The Barefooted Child* [cats. 41, 42, and 43]. Especially in the latter two of these, the aquatint is more painted than drawn. In *The Banjo Lesson* [cat. 40], she tried a very different technique. All of the color prints are colored à la poupée. Each plate is hand-colored with little "dolls" of rags, and the depth or strength of color is determined by how much ink is used. In the *Banjo Lesson* each impression was colored as a monotype with different dots on the skirt and pink and blue on the sleeves. The only printed areas aside from the drypoint lines were in the flesh tones and background tones for the skirts and the blouse. This made for very different results in each impression.

In accepting and incorporating Japanese influences into her style, Miss Cassatt enlarged its scope and attained added stature as an artist. With superior intelligence and taste she retained the very best elements of what she had learned earlier and added to them this enriching Japanese influence. Some further drypoints completed her graphic work into 1898 when she closed her studio, packed her trunks, and crossed the ocean for the first time since returning to Europe in 1872.

After her trip home where she visited family and friends for over six months, she divided her interests between her own work and helping her close friends, Mr. and Mrs. H. O. Havemeyer, and others to collect the paintings of her Impressionist colleagues. This became her great ambition and since art is selfish, her own painting and graphic work—which demanded complete concentration—suffered to some extent. There is, I think, less forceful precision and firmness of line such as is found in the graphic work done during her prime. There is freedom and rhythmic flow and an ease which is full of charm in those many little girls dressed up in various bonnets and plumed hats. She was encouraged to publish some of them in editions of fifty since there was now more demand for her work. She continued working in drypoint until about 1910 when the shiny surface of the copper plates began to hurt her eyes. Also with the death in 1911 of her brother Gardner, her last close relative, she had what might be called a nervous collapse which stopped all of her work for over two years. Her eyesight was failing; she had cataracts on both eyes and the operations were unsuccessful; by 1918 she could not distinguish objects. She often lamented the fact that in order to become an artist in her day, it had been necessary for her to leave her native land. By doing so, however, she made a unique place for herself in the art world as the only American within the Impressionist movement—a position she upheld with remarkable astuteness and graciousness.

Technical Methods Used by the Artist

Drypoint

Acid biting is never used to produce a drypoint. The polished copper plate may be smoked to make the drawing more distinct, but otherwise there is no coating applied. A needle—diamond point or other sharp tool—is drawn across the plate so that it actually cuts into the surface. As it penetrates tiny shavings of copper are raised on one or both sides of the line and a small furrow is made. It is this furrow on the sides of a drypoint line that gives it its characteristic appearance. When it is printed, ink lodges not only in the actual line made by the drypoint tool but is also held along the upraised edges of the furrow known as burr. When the plate is wiped preparatory to taking an impression, the ink held by the furrow is brushed along and feathered out, giving a soft, furry appearance to the printed line. The burr on a drypoint is very delicate and will wear off after very few impressions are pulled. Therefore, most editions of drypoints are limited to a small number.

Even in small editions the impressions vary. This is true of many of Miss Cassatt's drypoints; the first impressions taken being richly inked with much burr showing, the last having already lost the burr on the more delicate lines such as the shading on the faces and other flesh tones. In drypoints such as *Mrs. Gardner Cassatt and Her Baby Seated near a Window* [cat. 16] and *Baby's Back* [cat. 20] the wearing down of the most delicate burr is very obvious, even after some reinforcing during the course of the very small edition. In the case of the twenty-five restrikes of 1923, the reinforcing has created very spotty lines, giving the effect of very uneven inking.

Since Miss Cassatt used the drypoint process in order to teach herself to draw, the large majority of her prints, other than the series of twelve of 1889–1891 and about five others printed in an edition of twenty-five and one in an edition of fifty impressions, were printed in no more than five or six impressions. She thought of the majority of her prints as exercises, not finished works of art.

Hard-Ground Etching

In hard-ground etching, a plate—usually of copper—is coated with an acid-proof coating that, when dry, is hard to the touch. This ground is melted onto a hot plate—daubed or rolled on. The drawing is then done with a sharp tool—steel (sometimes with a diamond point), that scratches through the ground, exposing the metal surface. The plate is then put in an acid bath and the exposed metal is bitten away, leaving incised lines on the plate. The lines may be bitten from light to dark according to the varying lengths of time in the acid bath.

Soft-Ground Etching

In soft-ground etching, the metal plate—usually copper—is covered with a ground made up of hard-ground mixed with tallow or sometimes a grease such as vaseline. The mixture is made into a ball, often wrapped in a silk cloth, and a portion of it is then melted onto a heated plate. Over the plate, with soft-ground rolled or daubed on to cover it, is spread a sheet of drawing paper on which the artist sketches the design. The firm pressure of the pencil on the paper causes the soft-ground to adhere to the back of the paper so that the ground will pull away from the metal when the paper is lifted from the plate. The plate is thus exposed wherever the pencil has been drawn over the paper. The plate is then immersed in an acid bath for varied lengths of time according to the amount of ink to be held in the impression. The biting of the plate pits the surface of the areas drawn upon into ink pools which have a tendency to run together when closely juxtaposed.

The areas drawn are often outlines of figures; however, there may also be broad areas of tone similar to those bitten by aquatint, but demanding fewer steps in the process of printmaking. The areas to remain unbitten are stopped out with a brush dipped in a varnish usually made of a mixture of resin and alcohol. After one biting, lighter tones are then stopped out before a second biting where darker tones are wanted. This process can be repeated many times.

Aquatint

In the aquatint process, etching is done in tone rather than in line. It is mostly used with soft-ground or with straight etching or drypoint or with a combination of one or more of these processes. The aquatint ground may be laid in a number of different ways. Its main characteristics is that it is porous. It does not cover the surface of the plate completely and allows the acid to reach the metal through interstices between thousands of tiny resin dots. Instead of being an even coating of wax or tallow, aquatint ground is usually composed of particles of powdered resin dusted or sifted onto the surface of a plate and then heated. The resin may also be dissolved in alcohol spread over the plate, and as the solvent evaporates the resin particles are disposed on the surface of the metal as though they had been dusted on.

After the aquatint ground is laid, the sides and back of the plate are shellacked. All areas that are to remain white are stopped out with varnish, applied with a brush. (A grease pencil or crayon may also be used.) The plate is then immersed in a mordant bath. The acid reaches the metal between the resin particles and eats a tiny pocket around each of them. Light gray areas are bitten only a short time and then stopped out while darker areas are allowed a longer immersion in the acid.

Color Prints

Mary Cassatt's color prints are a masterful and unique contribution to the history of the graphic arts. Her entire graphic oeuvre reached a climax in the series of ten color prints first shown in 1891 in her first individual exhibition at Durand-Ruel's in Paris [cat. nos. 32-39]. The process she used for them is complicated, and her descriptions are rather puzzling. We have her written comments first in her letter to Samuel P. Avery of January 1903, and three years later in one to Frank Weiten-kampf. The intervening years—between twelve and fifteen since she had made any color prints—were a sufficiently long time to have caused her to forget the important part that soft-ground played in the description of the process. In the letter to Avery, she wrote:

> It is delightful to think that you take an interest in my work. I have sent with the set of my color etchings all of the 'states' I had. I wish I could have had more but I had to hurry on and be ready for my printer when I could get him. The printing is a great work; sometimes we worked all day (eight hours) both, as hard as we could work and only printed eight or ten proofs in the day. My method is very simple. I drew an outline in drypoint and transferred this to two other plates, making in all three plates, never more, for each proof. Then I put on aquatint wherever the color was to be printed; the color was painted on the plate as it was to appear in the proof. I tell you this because Mr. Lucas thought it might interest you and if any of the etchers in New York care to try the method you can tell them how it is done. I am anxious to know what you think of these new etchings. It amused me very much to do them although it was hard work.

In her letter of 1906 to Mr. Weitenkampf she wrote:

> I drew the outlines in drypoint and laid on a grain where color was to be applied, then colored à la poupée. I was entirely ignorant of the method when I began and as the plates were colored by me I varied sometimes the manner of applying the color. The set of ten plates was done with the intention of attempting an imitation of Japanese methods. Of course, I abandoned that somewhat after the first plate and tried more for atmosphere.

A close examination of the prints suggests, however, that the process was rather more complicated than that which Mary Cassatt described. The process of soft-ground etching seems to have played an important part. For this process, the copper plate is coated with a substance that resists acid but does not harden. The drawing is made on a sheet of paper placed over the plate, and the soft-ground adheres to the paper wherever the lines are drawn. These lines left in the soft-ground, which retain some of the texture of the paper, are then etched in the acid. In some cases, Cassatt was guided by such lightly etched soft-ground lines when she made her refined drypoint drawing on the plate. Using this method, the same drawing on paper could be used to transfer the image to the other plates that would be used for different colors.

Although some of the color tone was produced by aquatint, it is evident that the soft-ground technique also played a role. Sometimes the soft-ground was lifted by strokes on the overlying paper, and at times other textures were created on it. For some of the precise patterns, a stopping-out procedure was used in which the shapes were painted on the plate with an acid-resisting varnish.

When the plates were prepared through these various methods—soft-ground, drypoint, and aquatint—they were inked "à la poupée," that is, colored inks were dabbed onto the plates with "dolls" of rags. By separating color areas carefully, she was able not only to achieve particular brilliance but to combine more than one color on a single plate. Sometimes two plates were used, more often three. No more were necessary. Yet the range of hues in the finished prints was astonishingly wide and subtle.

Running these large plates through the press was a laborious job. To do this for the first set of ten color prints, Cassatt had the assistance of a printer named Le Roy, and she very generously included his name on the signature: "Imprimé par l'artiste et M. Le Roy."

It is of interest to know that no preliminary color sketches for the color prints have so far been recorded.

Notes

1. Frederick A. Sweet, *Miss Mary Cassatt, Impressionist from Pennsylvania* (Norman: University of Oklahoma Press, 1966), p. 57.
2. In French the word "gravures" refers to all incised techniques—etching, drypoint, and engraving.
3. Camille Pissarro, *Letters to his Son Lucien*, edited with the assistance of Lucien Pissarro by John Rewald (New York: Pantheon Books, Inc., 1943), p. 158.

Chronology

1844	Born May 22 at Allegheny City, Pennsylvania (now a part of Pittsburgh), second daughter and third child of Mr. and Mrs. Robert Simpson Cassatt.
1851–55	With her family to Paris, Heidelberg, and Darmstadt. Mary then learned both French and German at an early age.
1855	Robert (Robbie), the fourth child died in Darmstadt.
1855–66	Lived with her family in Philadelphia.
1861–66	Studied at The Pennsylvania Academy of the Fine Arts.
1866–70	With her mother to Paris, after which she remained there with friends. While in Paris, she studied with Charles Chaplin, Soyer, Couture, and Gérôme.
1868	Sent her painting *The Mandolin Player* to the Paris Salon where it was accepted.
1870–71	To Philadelphia to be with her family during the Franco-Prussian War.
1872	To Parma, Italy, where she studied graphic techniques with Carlo Raimondi. Stayed there eight months.
1873	Went from Rome to Madrid and Seville; then on to Antwerp and Haarlem where she copied a Franz Hals painting.
1874	Settled permanently in Paris.
1877	Her parents and sister Lydia came to live with her. Degas invited her to join the group then called "The Independents," later called "The Impressionists."
1879	Sent two light-filled paintings to the Fourth Impressionist Exhibition.

1880	Spent the summer at Marly-le-Roi in a villa next to that of Edouard Manet. Her brother Alexander brought his wife and four children for a long visit, and she charmed the three younger children into posing for her.
1882	In November, Lydia died of Bright's disease.
1883	Her younger brother Gardner brought his bride to visit the family.
1884	To Spain with her mother.
1887	Moved with her parents to an apartment at 10 Rue Marignan, Paris, which she kept for the rest of her life.
1890	She visited the Great Japanese Exhibition at the Ecole des Beaux Arts in Paris many times with Degas and other friends.
1890–91	She rented the Château Bachivillers on the Oise for the summer and fall, set up her etching press there and worked on the set of ten color prints.
1891	In April she had her first solo exhibition at Galerie Durand-Ruel, Paris. Her father died on December 9.
1892	Mrs. Potter Palmer commissioned her to execute a large mural for the World Columbian Exposition in Chicago.
1893	In November-December she held a much larger, more comprehensive exhibition of her paintings, pastels, drawings, and prints at Galerie Durand-Ruel, Paris, including fourteen color prints, the series of twelve drypoints, thirty-eight other prints, and one lithograph. She bought the Château de Beaufresne at Mesnil-Theribus, Oise, twenty-seven miles from Paris. It was her summer home for the rest of her life.
1895	In April her mother died. Durand-Ruel organized a Cassatt exhibition in their New York branch gallery, including eighteen prints.
1898–99	Her first visit to America since settling in Paris in 1874. She visited her brothers and their families as well as many good friends.
1901	Accompanied the Havemeyers to Italy and Spain and helped them to buy many fine paintings later given to the Metropolitan Museum of Art.

1904   Short trip to America. Guest of honor at the opening of the annual exhibition at the Chicago Art Institute in which she was offered a prize which she refused. She was made a Chevalier of the French Legion of Honor.

1908–09   Her last visit to America.

1910   Stopped her graphic work since the shiny copper plates hurt her eyes.

1910–11   To Egypt with the Gardner Cassatts. The death of Gardner Cassatt.

1911–12   Stopped painting and had the first operation for cataracts of both eyes.

1914   Awarded Gold Medal of Honor by The Pennsylvania Academy of The Fine Arts. Stopped her work in pastel due to progressive blindness. During World War I, spent most of her time at Grasse on the French Riviera.

1926   Died on June 14 at Château de Beaufresne.

CATALOG OF THE EXHIBITION

Dimensions are in inches with height preceding width and, unless otherwise indicated, are the plate size for each print. Centimeter measurements follow in parentheses.

Complete documentation, referred to as BR in each entry, can be found in the recently published *Mary Cassatt: A Catalogue Raisonné of the Graphic Work* (Washington, D.C.: Smithsonian Institution Press, 1980) by Adelyn Dohme Breeskin. This publication is an updated and greatly expanded revision of *The Graphic Work of Mary Cassatt* (New York: H. Bittner and Company, 1948), now out of print, by the same author.

The four color illustrations shown on the cover and pages 2, 6, and 12 are not repeated in the catalog.

1 **Costume Study after Gavarni**   c. 1878 or earlier
  Etching, drypoint, and aquatint
  8 x 5⅜ (20.3 x 13.6)   BR 2, third state
  Lent by Associated American Artists

2 **The Corner of the Sofa** (No. 3)   c. 1879
  Soft-ground and aquatint
  12³⁄₁₆ x 8¹¹⁄₁₆ (30.8 x 19.7)
  Plate destroyed   BR 16, third state
  Lent by The Art Institute of Chicago

3 **In the Opera Box** (No. 3)   c. 1880   [Also called *Au Théâtre*]   Soft-ground, aquatint, and etching
8⅛ x 7⅜ (20.4 x 18.7)   Plate destroyed   BR 22, fourth state   Lent by Indianapolis Museum of Art

4   **Woman Seated in a Loge**   c. 1880

[Also called *Au Théâtre*]
Lithograph on stone
11⁷⁄₁₆ x 8¾ (29 x 22.7)
Stone destroyed
BR 23, second state
Lent by The Baltimore Museum of Art

5   **Lady in Black, in a Loge, Facing Right**   c. 1880   [Also called *Au Spectacle*]   Soft-ground
7¾ x 11⁹⁄₁₆ (19.6 x 29.3)   BR 24, third state   Lent by The Library of Congress

6 **Knitting in the Library** c. 1881
Soft-ground and aquatint
10⅞ x 8⁹⁄₁₆ (29.4 x 22.8)   Plate destroyed
BR 30, third state
Lent by Treat Gallery, Bates College

7 **Knitting in the Glow of a Lamp**
c. 1880   Soft-ground
11⁵⁄₁₆ x 9 (29.4 x 27.8)
BR 31, second state
Lent by Grand Rapids Art Museum

8   **The Visitor**   c. 1880   [Also called *Scene d'Interieur*]
    Soft-ground, aquatint, etching, drypoint, and fabric texture   15⅝ x 12³⁄₁₆ (39.9 x 31)   BR 34, fourth state
    Lent by The Library of Congress

9 **Mlle Luguet Seated on a Couch** c. 1883
Soft-ground and aquatint 8½ x 5½ (21.9 x 14.2)
BR 49, second state
Lent by The Library of Congress

10 **Susan Seated before a Row of Trees** c. 1883
Etching and drypoint 9³⁄₁₆ x 6½ (23.3 x 16.5)
BR 54, only known state
Lent by Associated American Artists

11 **Mrs. Cassatt Reading to Her Grandchildren** (No. 1)
c. 1880 Soft-ground 6⅛ x 11¾ (16.2 x 22.2)
BR 58, third state Lent by Smith College Museum of Art

12 Lydia Reading, Turned toward Right
c. 1881   Soft-ground and aquatint
7¹⁄₁₆ x 4¾ (18 x 11)   BR 63, second state
Lent by Smith College Museum of Art

16 Nurse and Baby Bill (No. 2)   c. 1889
Soft-ground with netting texture
8⅝ x 5½ (21.6 x 13.7)   BR 109, second state
Lent by The Baltimore Museum of Art

14 Elsie Holding a Cat, Looking Left   c. 1884
Drypoint   9⅜ x 6⁵⁄₁₆ (23.7 x 16.3)
BR 89, only known state
Lent by The Minneapolis Institute of Arts

13 **Reading the Newspaper** (No. 2)   c. 1882   Soft-ground and aquatint   5⅜ x 6½ (14.3 x 16.5)
BR 73, second state   Lent by The Art Institute of Chicago

15 **Young Girl Fixing Her Hair** (No. 1)   c. 1889   Drypoint
8⅜ x 6¼ (21.2 x 15.8)   BR 99, third state   Lent by The Library of Congress

17 **Gardner Held by His Mother**   c. 1887   Drypoint   8¼ x 5⁷⁄₁₆ (20.9 x 13.8)
BR 113, only known state   Lent by Cooper-Hewitt Museum of Design and Decorative Arts

18   **A Portrait of the Artist's Mother**   c. 1889   Soft-ground and aquatint   9⅞ x 7¹/₁₆ (25 x 17.9)
BR 122, seventh state   Lent by Museum of Art, Carnegie Institute

19 **The Map** 1890 [Also called *The Lesson*] Drypoint 6³⁄₁₆ x 9³⁄₁₆ (15.7 x 23.3) Plate destroyed
BR 127, third state Lent by The Art Institute of Chicago

20 **Baby's Back**   1890   Drypoint, with a few soft-ground lines   9³⁄₁₆ x 6⁷⁄₁₆ (23 x 16.3)
Plate destroyed   BR 128, third state   Lent by The Baltimore Museum of Art

21 **The Stocking** 1890   Drypoint   10¼ x 7⁵⁄₁₆ (26 x 18.5)   Plate destroyed   BR 129, fifth state
Lent by The Art Museum, Princeton University

22 **The Mandolin Player**   c. 1889   Drypoint   9⅛ x 6⅜ (23.7 x 16.2)   Plate destroyed
BR 130, seventh state   Lent by Hackley Art Museum

23 **Reflection** c. 1890   Drypoint   10³⁄₁₆ x 6⅞ (25.8 x 17.4)
Plate destroyed   BR 131, fourth state
Lent by The Brooklyn Museum

24 **Repose** c. 1890   Drypoint   9¼ x 6⁹⁄₁₆ (23.6 x 16.8)
Plate destroyed   BR 132, fifth state   Lent by Springfield Art Museum

25 **Tea** c. 1890   Drypoint   7⅙ x 6⅛ (17.9 x 15.5)   Plate destroyed
BR 133, fifth state   Lent by Grand Rapids Art Museum

26 **Hélène of Septeuil** c. 1890   [Also called *Enfant au Perroquet*]
Drypoint   9⅜ x 6³⁄₁₆ (24 x 16)   Plate destroyed
BR 134, fifth state   Lent by Treat Gallery, Bates College

27 **Nursing** c. 1890   Drypoint $9\frac{5}{8}$ x 7 (23.8 x 17.7)
Plate destroyed   BR 135, third state
Lent by The Library of Congress

28 **The Mirror** c. 1891 Drypoint 8⅞ x 6¹¹⁄₁₆ (22.8 x 17)
Plate destroyed BR 136, sixth state
Lent by Grand Rapids Art Museum

29　**The Bonnet**　c. 1891　　Drypoint　　7¼ x 5⁷⁄₁₆ (18.4 x 13.8)　　Plate destroyed　　BR 137, third state
Lent by The Brooklyn Museum

30 **The Parrot** c. 1891   Drypoint   6⅜ x 4¹¹⁄₁₆ (16.2 x 12)   Plate destroyed
BR 138, sixth state   Lent by The Art Museum, Princeton University

31 **Quietude** c. 1891   Drypoint   10¹⁄₁₈ x 6¼ (25.3 x 17)   Plate destroyed   BR 139, fifth state
Anonymous lender

32 **The Bath** c. 1891 [Also called *The Tub*] Color print with drypoint and soft-ground
12⁵⁄₁₆ x 9¹³⁄₁₆ (31.2 x 25) BR 143, eleventh and final state
Lent by Museum of Art, Carnegie Institute

33 In the Omnibus c. 1891 [Also called *The Tramway*] Color print with drypoint and soft-ground
14⅚₁₆ x 10½ (36.6 x 26.7) BR 145, fourth and final state Lent by Museum of Art, Carnegie Institute

36 **The Coiffure** c. 1891   Color print with drypoint and soft-grained   14⅜ x 10½ (36.7 x 26.7)
BR 152, fourth and final state   Lent by Georgia Museum of Art, the University of Georgia

37 **Mother's Kiss** c. 1891   Color print with drypoint and soft-ground   13⅝ x 8¹⁵⁄₁₆ (34.5 x 22.7)
BR 149, fourth and final state   Lent by Museum of Art, Carnegie Institute

40 **The Banjo Lesson** c. 1893   Color print with drypoint and soft-ground   11⅝ x 9⅜ (29.5 x 24.7)
Plates destroyed   BR 156, fourth state   Lent by Grand Rapids Art Museum

41 Gathering Fruit c. 1893   [Also called *l'Espalier*]   Color print with drypoint and aquatint
16¾ x 11¾ (42.5 x 29.8)   BR 157, fifth and final state   Lent by The Library of Congress

42 **Peasant Mother and Child** c. 1894 Color print with drypoint and aquatint $11^{11}/_{16}$ x $9^{5}/_{16}$ (29.6 x 23.6)
BR 159, fourth state Lent by Associated American Artists

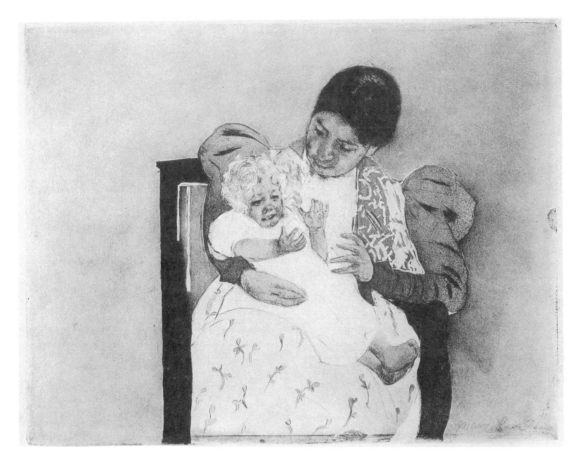

43 **The Barefooted Child**   c. 1898   Color print with drypoint and aquatint
9½ x 12⁷⁄₁₆ (24.1 x 31.5)   BR 160, third state   Lent by Grand Rapids Art Museum

44 **The Crocheting Lesson**   c. 1902   Drypoint
17⁵⁄₁₆ x 10½ (45 x 26.6)   Plate destroyed
BR 178, second state   Lent by Treat Gallery, Bates College

45 **Margot Wearing a Bonnet** (No. 1)   c. 1902
Drypoint printed in color
9³⁄₁₆ x 6½ (23.3 x 16.5)
BR 179, only known state
Lent by Delaware Art Museum

46 **Margot Wearing a Bonnet** (No. 3)   c. 1902
Drypoint   9 x 6¼ (22.8 x 15.8)
BR 181, only known state
Lent by Grand Rapids Art Museum

47 **The Party Dress**   c. 1904   Drypoint
8³⁄₁₆ x 5⅞ (20.8 x 15)   BR 191, second state
Lent by Treat Gallery, Bates College

48 **Mother Holding Her Nude Baby** c. 1900
Drypoint   8⅛ x 5¹¹⁄₁₆ (20.6 x 14.4)
BR 206, second state
Lent by Treat Gallery, Bates College

50 **Looking into the Hand Mirror** (No. 3)   c. 1905
Drypoint   8¾ x 5¼ (21 x 14.5)
BR 202+, only known state
(+ designates recently found print)
Lent by Adelyn D. Breeskin

49   **Denise Holding Her Child by Both Hands**   c. 1908   Drypoint
16 x 11¼ (40.6 x 28.5)   BR 208, second state
Lent by Treat Gallery, Bates College

This book was produced by the Smithsonian Institution Press, Washington, D.C.

Printed by Schneidereith & Sons Printers.

Set in 12/16 Palatino Linotype by Service Composition.

The text paper is 80 lb. Karma Natural

with 80 lb. Karma Natural cover

and Multicolor endpapers.

Designed by Elizabeth Sur.